The BIRD Way

A Simple Practice for Finding Lightness in a Heavy World

By: Forest of Truth

Copyright © 2025 Forest of Truth

Published by Forest of Truth, an Imprint of Witty Wizard LLC

All rights reserved.

No part of this publication may be reproduced, distributed, or transmitted in any form or by any means: electronic, mechanical, photocopying, recording, or otherwise, without prior written permission from the publisher, except in the case of brief quotations used in reviews or critical articles.

This book contains original text and illustrations created with the assistance of artificial intelligence (AI). All images and text have been significantly edited, enhanced, and finalized by hand using digital illustration and word processing tools. This work reflects the author's creative vision and artistic decisions. This work constitutes human authorship and is protected under U.S. and international copyright laws.

Disclaimer:
This book is based on personal experience, reflection, and opinion.
It is intended for educational and inspirational purposes only and is not a substitute for professional medical, psychological, or therapeutic advice. Seek care from qualified professionals as needed.

Introduction:

Do you want to live like a bird: light, soaring, and singing through life? It sounds wonderful, doesn't it? Maybe right now you're hoping it will be easy. Or maybe it sounds impossible for you. Well, I'd suggest it's neither.

Living like a bird isn't about pretending life is always easy or light. It's not a fantasy, it's a practice. Birds face storms, predators, and harsh winters. They work hard to survive. But still, they fly. Still, they sing. And still, they appear weightless as they soar through the open sky.

The point here is that sustainable change requires balance. If you want to soar high, you must be willing to go deep. If you want to feel light, you must first understand the weight you've been carrying so you can release it. And if you want to sing again, you need to face your challenges with clarity and courage, so they no longer drown out your song.

The BIRD Way establishes a practice that can help you shift your way of being.

This book gives you a framework to reference during life's heavier moments, not by avoiding them, but by engaging them directly with clarity and compassion. It's about giving yourself a foundation that supports your ability to naturally experience more of the happiness, lightness, and freedom you long for.

Here's how it works:

- **Breathe**: Come back to the present moment and your body.
- **Investigate**: With honesty and gentleness, explore what's really going on inside.
- **Redirect**: Shift your focus and energy to align with what truly serves you.
- **Decide**: Take clear, intentional steps forward with full commitment.

This is *The BIRD Way*. It's a way of living that can guide you not only through hard moments, but toward a more open, vibrant, and joyful version of your life.

Part I:
Understanding Your Cage

Chapter 1: The Illusion of Lightness

We often look at people who seem carefree and assume they've figured out something we haven't. Maybe they were just born lighter, or luckier. Maybe their lives are just easier. Maybe they've never been through what you have. That could be true in some cases. It could be false in others. Sometimes we see people who seem to have figured it out, and don't know they have been through tremendous struggle. Or that they are still juggling challenges today but finding joy in their lives despite them. Either way, it's our beliefs that impact us the most. If we stick with the belief that lightness is either natural but not for us, or generally unattainable, it becomes one of the greatest illusions keeping us stuck.

True lightness isn't about avoiding struggle. It's not about pretending everything's okay or smiling through pain. In fact, trying to *act* light while feeling heavy only deepens the disconnection inside. However, if you have heavy moments in your life, but find ways to adapt, change, or at times even accept the circumstances; it creates room for other feelings to have their own moments despite your challenges.

Birds don't fly by denying gravity. They fly by working within its pull.

In the same way, if you want to live with lightness, you must acknowledge the forces that pull you down. This gives you more power, from which you can then build the strength and wisdom to rise anyway. If the bird believed: "Eagles fly up to mountains, so it must be easy" and tried to fly off a cliff on its first try, it might not go well. If a bird decided: "Gravity exists, I won't ever be able to fly" it wouldn't ever try leaving the nest. But nature finds a balance, so they know they can, and they know how to stay aware of their limits in different situations.

However, we humans live in a culture that oversimplifies positivity and idolizes speed: *just think positive, manifest better, be successful*. But this mindset can cause more harm than good. It teaches us to skip over our truth, to repress the parts of ourselves that need compassion and clarity. It also implies that we must be at the top of the mountain to be happy, when happiness can be found in the smallest moments. I've participated in many training programs that have been helpful to me over the years. In one I had the chance to speak to a millionaire, and when he asked me "How's it going?", I naturally replied: "Well I'm in a hammock, so I'm living the dream". I said it playfully, and while I was also excited to learn and generate more income guided by his experience, it also came from a place of genuine meaning. Reflecting later, I noticed this response was from living a practice of appreciating the little things.

Simultaneously, many of us are taught limiting beliefs by the world around us. It's usually from a place of care. Parents, wanting the best for their children, often encourage us to be careful, play it safe, and avoid risk. For them and others, this caution may even turn into pessimism over time. Sometimes people challenge this dynamic, but don't stick with it through the difficulties, and then become jaded. But it doesn't have to be that way. Understanding that gravity exists doesn't limit the birds, and it shouldn't hold us back either. Now, I know some of you might be thinking *sure birds can fly, but humans can't*. I challenge you to remember that someone invented airplanes. A lot of people must have dismissed that idea before it was made tangible.

Birds don't skip over anything. They navigate winds. They rest on branches when tired. They build nests for safety and protection. Lightness, for them, isn't something they fake, it's something they earn through their growth, consistency, and trust in the moment. The same is possible for us.

Lightness comes not from suppressing your pain, but from understanding it. It comes from letting go of what isn't yours to carry, which is much easier to do after you're sure you've integrated the lessons available from the experience. And most of all, it comes from learning how to move through the world in a way that honors yourself and others, not just your image.

In the chapters ahead, you'll learn how to stop chasing lightness like a mood or mask, and instead, create it from within. The BIRD Way isn't about becoming someone new. It's about unlearning the lie that you must carry everything alone, pretend to be okay, or rise above all difficulty. The illusion of lightness will keep you chasing something fake.

The practice of grounding, aligning to your truth, and building up gratitude will invite moments of lightness into your heart. Next, let's look at what is weighing you down.

Chapter 2: What's Weighing You Down?

Before we can feel light, we must understand what's making us heavy.

Many of us carry more than we realize: unspoken grief, inherited expectations, and unconscious fears. These old beliefs operate so quickly, we start to accept them as our foundation, which limits what we can build. We stop questioning them, because these thoughts have run so many times in our mind they are now on autopilot. These weights don't always show up as dramatic breakdowns or even appear unusual. Often, they appear as the slow, quiet drain on our energy: procrastination, emotional numbness, self-doubt, tension in the body, or the feeling that we're never quite present where we are. We might feel that we were meant to be *someone else*, but we aren't someone else, so we're *stuck* being who we are now.

You don't have to have gone through obvious trauma to feel this way. Even ordinary life can stack up: the things we were subtly taught to hide, the pressure to be perfect, the fear of being misunderstood, the exhaustion of holding it all together. We also often forget about things that were hard in our childhoods. The things we didn't have the energy to process, because we were still vulnerable and inexperienced. There are things that we may have locked away just to get through that time. This walling away of difficulties is the best we knew how to do at the time, but without resolution, we can still be carrying that weight.

These burdens are real. And yet, they often live in our blind spots. We normalize them, or other people normalize them to us. We are told, "That is just life," or "Other people have it worse," or "You should be able to handle this."

But the truth is, anything you carry without space to process will eventually become draining. We can only carry so much at a time. It's obvious in the physical world but is often overlooked emotionally. The good news is that noticing and choosing to start unpacking these emotional burdens can drastically change the feelings that start to build up over time. We need to be patient with ourselves in the process though, this didn't build up overnight and likely the amount of change we want to see won't happen overnight either. But it's still worth pursuing.

This chapter is an invitation to gently and honestly look at what's weighing you down. Not to blame or dwell, but to witness, name, and begin loosening your grip on things that no longer serve you.

Start here:

- What emotional weight do you feel in your body right now?
- What patterns or thoughts seem to keep repeating in your mind lately?
- What have you been avoiding because it feels too heavy?
- Where do you feel pressure to be someone you are not?
- What is holding you back from being who you really are?

Don't try to fix it all right now. This isn't about solving everything, it's about becoming more comfortable with speaking your truth. Even when it's not comfortable, being willing to do it, building courage and strength.

Journaling these questions can help you identify the invisible chains that keep you from rising. As you bring them into awareness, you create new possibilities. Remember: birds don't fly because there's no gravity, they fly because they've learned how to respond to it. The first step of responding to it… is noticing it.

In the next chapter, we'll explore how facing heaviness is not a contradiction to lightness, but the path to it. The deeper you go, the higher you can rise.

Chapter 3: Why Flight Requires Depth

It's tempting to think that to feel better, we should just "move on." Rise above. Let it go. Stay light. Stay happy. But real flight, real freedom, doesn't come from skipping over our pain. It comes from moving through it. From adapting to an environment that isn't always easy. From becoming capable of navigating different challenges in a way that makes us resilient. In time, we know that we have the depth and capacity to do what we need to, which gives us the courage to take the leaps towards the things we want most in our lives.

Birds don't fly by simply floating away from the earth. They push against it. They trust themselves even to give into gravity at times, and dive. They rest and rise again. Their lightness isn't the absence of struggle; it's the result of adaptation and instinct.

In the same way, when we try to avoid what's heavy: our grief, fear, shame, or unmet needs, we don't become lighter. We become split. Part of us wants to rise, but another part is still grasping at ways to avoid the blockers that haven't even been acknowledged.

This split shows up in our lives as inner conflict, burnout, or confusion. Our energy and focus are scattered, possibly resulting in cycles of trying something and then giving up. We feel like we're flapping our wings without gaining any lift. That's because we're trying to fly without depth.

This can start to feel like there is some invisible barrier that applies to us, and that we won't ever be able to break through it. But you can, you will first have to see it for what it is. When you illuminate the barrier, you can find a way beyond it. Whether that is brute force applied to burst through it, consistently chipping away at the same spot, or a path around it, any approach becomes simpler and more realistic once it's visible.

To rise in any lasting way, we must build from something real. Depth gives us the opportunity to form a new foundation. It's the process of being honest with ourselves, acknowledging where we've been, and allowing ourselves to feel what's true. It's about being willing to be imperfect, and practicing compassion with ourselves and others. To look at ugly things and know this willingness helps us improve. To think less like: "How am I still stuck?", and instead more like: "I'm feeling disappointed that I'm still limited by this challenge, but I'm going to find a way. I'm proud I'm being this honest about it and doing the work."

Depth means:

- Being willing to sit with discomfort.
- Being honest, even if you don't like what you find.
- Facing what you've been afraid to feel.
- Listening to your own story with compassion.

None of this is easy to do, but it is powerful. The paradox is: the more you learn to go inward, the more freedom you'll feel taking action outward. Like roots strengthening a tree, your inner work supports your outer growth.

If you want to soar, you don't need to escape yourself. You need to meet yourself more fully where you are now, even if that means a spotlight shines on what you don't like about yourself today. When you do this work, you'll find that you are actually stronger than the heaviness you feared. Once you become able to lift that weight, it can't stay or hold you back. There is a payoff after all this work. One day you will look back and notice it simply was there before, and then you moved it out of your way. It was there to teach you how to fly.

In the next part of the book, we'll walk through the four practices of *The BIRD Way*. These actions provide grounded steps that help you stay calm, think more clearly, and move forward with more intention.

Part II:
The BIRD Way

Chapter 4: Breathe

Every journey begins with a breath. Not always a conscious breath, but still, a breath. When it is a conscious breath however, it's even more invigorating. It tells your body and your mind, "I'm here." It tells both: there is a part of you that is here, that hears you. The awareness within you that is experiencing this life, wants to connect with you. And as these pieces of you start to communicate again, you become more connected, awake, and aligned.

Before birds take flight, they pause. They scan the wind and steady themselves. This stillness is not hesitation, its presence. And presence is strongly connected to the breath. If you don't believe it, just try taking 6 deep breaths and notice how you feel. There is a lot of hype out there, but there aren't many things that you can get firsthand evidence for yourself in less than a minute or two. When breathing deeply and slowly, you can see that it has an impact on your state of consciousness nearly immediately. Imagine what it can do over time, if you integrate it into a practice.

When life feels overwhelming, breath can become your anchor. When your thoughts race or emotions surge, you can always come back to something simple and steady: the inhale, and the exhale. It's always available. At any moment, you can access your breath. It might not always feel like what you want to do. In a survival situation, it might not make sense to take these types of breaths. So, when you are in fight or flight mode, it might not feel natural. However, it's also not natural to be in an environment that puts us into fight or flight mode so much of the time.

But most of us have learned to hold our breath. We are overstimulated and exhausted, so we tense up, brace ourselves, and force ourselves to hold onto any reserves we can. Without realizing it, we disconnect from our bodies and the moment we're in. We stop filling our lungs completely and accidentally limit our ability to fill ourselves with the very energy we need. We limit our ability to take in, and as a result, also our ability to let go.

To live like a bird, we must reconnect with our breath. Not just as a physical act, but as a practice of recharging, embracing life, and moving forward.

<u>Technique #1 - Box breathing:</u>

- Inhale slowly through your nose for 4 seconds
- Hold your breath for 4 seconds
- Exhale slowly through your mouth for 4 seconds
- Hold again for 4 seconds before breathing in again
- Repeat this pattern as long as you wish to continue

Technique #2 - 6 Way Breathing:

First: start with a practice round of breathing in three directions within your body: first your belly, then your ribs, and finally your upper chest.

- Inhale slowly through your nose and expand downward into your belly.
- Keep inhaling and allow this breath to fill outwards, letting your ribs expand in all directions.
- Finish your inhale by gently allowing the air to fill into your upper chest.

Hold briefly, if it feels comfortable.

- Exhale slowly pushing the air up from your belly.
- Then let your ribs soften inward.
- Finally, gently contract your belly to finish releasing all of the air.

Repeat a few times, following the same three-part wave in and out.

In any moment these techniques can serve as a simple tool to calm your system and return you to center. With practice, either can make your natural breathing become easier and fuller over time. This has many benefits, as deep breathing moves your body differently, and wakes up mechanisms that help you to heal.

Other helpful practices include:

- **Grounded Breathing**: Placing one hand on your chest, one on your belly, and noticing as they rise.
- **Sighing Out**: Letting out a natural sigh when tension builds, signaling safety to your system.
- **Soft Focus Breathing**: Looking at something gently while breathing slowly, helping you ground into your environment.

The point isn't to breathe "right", or to find the most optimized breathing method. It's to breathe *intentionally*. To remind yourself that you have a choice in how you meet each moment. It's to reconnect with the different parts of you, allowing you to have more control over how you respond to your life.

Breath can be your reset button. When you want to choose how you are going to navigate or respond to something in life, arriving here in this breath creates space for that evaluation and choice.

In the next chapter, we'll build on this foundation. We now can utilize this space when challenges arise, to begin to investigate what's really going on internally.

Chapter 5: Investigate

Once you've grounded yourself with your breath, you have created enough stillness to look inward. This initiates the next step, *Investigate*. The purpose is to see clearly first, in order understand how you can approach making intentional shifts. This includes noticing when your perception has been focused through a lens of fear or habit, and doing so with curiosity, honesty, and compassion. It also means seeking clarity on what we really want, and why. This step of the process is required, to enable you to make lasting changes through the steps that follow.

To live like a bird is not to ignore life's chaotic attributes, but instead to move through them with awareness and grace. Birds don't try to control the wind; they feel it, respond to it, and adjust course as necessary. Investigating your internal habits, desires, and beliefs, hearing your inner voice and asking: *is this what I want to be focusing on,* is your version of that attunement.

Too often, we move through life reacting unconsciously. We feel anxious and try to suppress it. We feel angry and lash out or shut down. We don't usually stop to ask: *What's really going on here? Where is this coming from? What do I need?*

Investigation is not an interrogation or asking with a tone of critical self-judgement. It's not about overthinking or analyzing yourself endlessly. It's about noticing, listening, and asking with a purpose; to better understand, acknowledge, and empower change.

Here are some gentle questions to begin with:

- What emotion am I feeling right now, underneath the noise?
- Is this feeling familiar? When have I felt it before?
- What story am I telling myself about this situation?
- What part of me is asking to be heard or healed?

You can journal your answers, speak them aloud, or simply sit with them. The point is not to "solve" everything, it's to build a relationship with your inner world to get increasingly more leverage on your beliefs and actions.

Think of this step like a bird learning the air currents. The more you pay attention, the more skillfully you can move. The more you ignore it, the more you get tossed around.

Here are a few supportive practices for this phase:

- **Emotion Naming**: Instead of staying at a general description like "I feel bad," try to name the specific emotion: grief, fear, guilt, shame, anger, worry, etc.
- **Inner Dialoguing**: Write a conversation with a part of yourself, like your inner child or your inner critic. Ask them questions about what drives their fears and behaviors.
- **Pattern Mapping**: Track recurring reactions or triggers and ask what belief or experience might be beneath them. Notice improvements you have made before and the patterns that have formed as a result.

Remember, this is not about perfection. Some days you'll go deeper in your analysis. Some days you'll only scratch the surface. Both are part of the work. When you ask these types of questions, or listen carefully to your inner voice, you create space to notice areas for improvement. Sometimes an intense month with a lot of self-work leads to seemingly no results, then when things finally calm down, you have a life-shifting realization seemingly out of nowhere. But it wasn't out of nowhere, you had already laid the groundwork.

Stay kind, curious, and disciplined with yourself. Investigation isn't easy, but it's a call to action within ourselves to seek areas for growth.

In the next chapter, we'll explore how to take what you've discovered and begin redirecting it, toward something that serves you rather than something that feels familiar. That's how you shift your flight path and ultimately engage differently with your life.

Chapter 6: Redirect

Once you've paused to breathe and taken the time to investigate what's happening within, you stand at a powerful turning point. You're no longer reacting automatically, you're choosing how to respond. This is the moment to *Redirect*.

Birds don't fly in straight lines. They move with the wind. They rise on thermals, adjust course mid-air, and shift their direction when needed. Redirection is not failure, it's adaptation. It doesn't mean we have to focus on how what we've done so far is *bad*, it just means that we want to go somewhere we weren't previously headed. This simply requires action and a change in course.

In our lives, we often assume we must keep going the way we've been going. We think, "This is just how I am," or "It's too late to change." But the truth is: once you see clearly, you can steer more accurately. The reason we get the same results is because we repeat the same habits. When you shift your attention, your energy, and your response, your direction and outcomes change as well.

Redirecting is not about denying where you have been or what you might feel about it. It's not about suppressing emotions or pretending you are someone you aren't. It's about deciding where to go next and putting more of your energy in that direction. You are not running away from what you don't like, but instead you are choosing what you want to move towards. You are acknowledging where and who you currently are, and choosing where you are going and who you are becoming. This happens through your beliefs and actions from this moment on.

Let's say you've investigated and discovered that you struggle with feelings of anxiety that stem from a fear of failure. You might still feel that fear coming up at times, but now, you don't have to freeze, get frustrated, or avoid it. Instead, you can acknowledge it and then *redirect* your focus toward courage, your energy toward preparation, and your attention toward what you *can* control.

Redirection begins with intention. Ask:

- What am I choosing to focus on right now?
- Where is my energy going?
- What beliefs support the person I want to become?
- How can I act in alignment with my values, what actions would I take?

This doesn't mean suppressing what's real. It means partnering with your mind, within your current reality, and guiding yourself toward a better outcome one step at a time.

Try this practice:

1. **Name** the emotion or pattern you've identified.
2. **Validate** it with compassion: "It makes sense I feel this way, given these experiences."
3. **Choose** to move forward: "I am ready for a new experience, and this new focus will support more feelings that help me achieve this change."

4. **Reiterate** with consistent small shifts: a thought, a question, an action, or even a posture that moves you one degree in a better direction. Redirection doesn't happen all at once; it happens from compounding choices and continuing in the new direction.

Examples:

- From scrolling endlessly, to stepping outside or focusing on breathing for a few minutes.

- From "I'm overwhelmed," to "I can do the first thing on my priority list."

- From "I always fail," to "I'm learning and improving with practice."

Redirection is not dramatic. It's steady. Like a bird staying in the air, one flap of its wings at a time. And when practiced consistently, these small shifts begin to create new patterns. Over time, you no longer live automatically following old habits, instead you begin flying your chosen course.

In the next chapter, we'll talk about how to take this momentum and channel it into clear, grounded decision-making. That is how your inner shift creates real-world outcomes.

Chapter 7: Decide

After you've grounded yourself in breath, investigated what's happening, and gently redirected your focus, you're ready for the final step in the BIRD Way: *Decide*.

In the last chapter we looked at your thoughts, or your internal world. Your focus certainly impacts your outcomes, but when it comes down to it, you won't ever have complete control of all your thoughts. We have thousands a day. While practicing more iterations of thoughts that support us does go a long way in making this natural, the area you do always have full control of is your external actions. This is where decision comes into play.

Deciding is not about having it all figured out. It's about making a *clear, grounded choice* in the present moment, for how you are going to interact with the external world. It's a commitment, not to perfection, but to what you have chosen to act on. When you make a choice aligned to living in accordance with what you value, you will be more likely to follow through. If you haven't followed through on something before, it does not mean you can't. It simply means you previously didn't commit to the right things, or you didn't work through the resistance that came up. This time, you did the investigation, the redirection, and you are now ready to decide with depth and thus full commitment.

Birds don't hesitate forever before leaping from a branch. They sense the wind, trust their wings, and take flight. They don't know where every gust of wind will carry them, but they go. Similarly, you don't need certainty to take your next step. You just need enough clarity to act with intention. If the clarity of the direction you chose has sufficient depth, why would you want to do anything different than what you've committed to?

The world often tells us to wait for the right mood, the right time, the right answer. But waiting too long keeps us trapped in indecision, which can feel heavier than starting in a new direction and shaping our path as we go. Deciding lightens the load. We know what the next step is, and we already know we are taking it. Deciding doesn't mean rigidity, or that you can't change anything again. It means you aren't going to make excuses or hold yourself back from the things that matter most to you anymore.

Here are some ways to practice intentional decision-making:

- **Check In with Your Values**
  Ask: "Is this decision aligned with the kind of life I want to build?"

- **Choose Progress Over Perfection**
  Small decisions, made with integrity, build momentum. Don't underestimate them.

- **Use the 'Next Right Step' Approach**
  You don't need to know the whole path. You just need to take the next step that feels true.

- **Create a Decision Ritual**
  You might light a candle, take a deep breath, or write your decision down as a promise to yourself. Ritual helps signal commitment to your body and mind.

Deciding doesn't mean everything becomes easy. But it does mean you're no longer drifting, you're steering. You're declaring to yourself: "I choose to engage with life, here's how" and that clarity leads to commitment. When you truly decide, you will follow through. As a result, you build trust in yourself and claim a little more of your freedom.

You're not meant to hover on the edge of what your life could be. You're meant to leap into it.

In the next section of the book, we'll explore what it looks like to live this way. Moving through the world with presence, resilience, and joy.

You've learned the BIRD Way. Now let's look at what life can be like, when you live it.

Part III:
Living Like a Bird

Chapter 8: Singing Anyway

Birds don't only sing when the skies are clear. They sing at dawn after long nights. They sing after storms as the skies calm and conditions ease. They sing not because life is perfect, but because it's *their experience of life*. Their song is a response to presence, an opportunity to celebrate the existence of this moment.

This chapter is about reclaiming your joy. Not as a reward for surviving or a prize for fixing everything, but as something you're allowed to access *right now*, even as you continue to grow.

We often withhold joy from ourselves without even noticing it. We think things like, "I'll feel good when I finish healing," or "I'll let myself be happy once I've solved this problem." Life isn't something you win after completing certain objectives. It's a series of moments, opportunities, successes, struggles, and many gifts to be grateful for, both large and small. This ranges from the obvious like people and animals you care about, down to the simplicities like the feeling of the sun warming your face, when you take your coffee outside in the morning.

If you keep waiting for the perfect moment to feel contentment or gratitude, you will miss out on little moments where joy is already possible. It might look different to you, but we all have some space in our life we can welcome appreciation into our hearts. The more you practice this, the more easily it will come.

To sing anyway means:

- Smiling even when you don't have it all figured out.
- Letting yourself dance, even if you don't know what to do with your arms.
- Laughing, even though you haven't found a way to resolve all your pain.

Welcoming joy doesn't mean you're ignoring the hard parts of your life, or that you have certainty there won't be new challenges even if you do find a way to address the current ones. It means you're not letting them define your whole experience.

This is what it looks like to live like a bird. To let yourself be lifted by small wonders, a beam of sunlight, the sound of leaves, a kind word, a hug. To recognize that joy is not something you can only afford later. It's free, it's reachable now, and it's healing. It's part of what keeps us rising and makes the hardships of life worth facing.

Try this:

- Every day, make space to notice at least one moment of beauty.
- Practice welcoming joy, pausing to seek what could feel good in the moment.
- Allow yourself to smile or laugh even if the inspiration doesn't *make sense*.

If joy feels far away, start small. Just notice what softens your body. What brings a breath of ease. Sometimes life does throw us challenges, and it can take some time for your song to begin again. The point is to welcome it back, so as you become ready and the skies let some light through, you can create these moments.

But remember, you don't need to wait until everything is fixed to feel positive emotions. You can even sing in the storm if you want to. Joy, love, and play are all immensely healing. They can support your growth as you learn, experiment, try, fail, improve, and succeed throughout life.

In the next chapter, we will explore what to do when the winds shift. This means learning how to stay steady and resilient, even when life throws you off course. Because living like a bird doesn't mean avoiding the storms. It means learning how to fly through them.

Chapter 9: Feathers in the Storm

We have already established that living like a bird doesn't mean life becomes easy. However, as you learn how to stay steady yourself when the sky turns dark, it can in some ways become easier. You don't control the wind, but you can adjust your wings. The more wise, adaptable, and strong you become, the less these challenges weigh on you.

Storms will come. Some you will see forming. Others might hit without warning. These moments, when things get rough, grief rises, or fear returns, are where the BIRD Way becomes more than a practice. It becomes a support system.

Resilience doesn't mean bouncing back perfectly. It means *staying connected to yourself* even when things feel out of control. It means having a choice in how you respond. It means remembering that you've faced hard things before, and that you have tools now you didn't have back then.

In stormy moments, it's easy to forget the path. So, here's a reminder:

- **Breathe**: Come back to your body. It starts with the first breath.

- **Investigate**: Practice curiosity in what's happening beneath the surface.

- **Redirect**: Find the shifts you can make now: your focus, your goal, your next word.

- **Decide**: Choose your actions, even if it's just through the next hour.

This framework isn't limited to use only exactly as described above. Sometimes you may forget to breathe and find yourself deep in investigation. You can go back into your breath at any step, and it will still serve you. You may start by deciding you will make a change in a moment with deep conviction, and the other steps can help make the new path easier to stay on, or smoother to follow.

Think of a bird caught in a storm. It doesn't fly higher into chaos. It finds shelter and waits. It conserves energy and rides it out. You will still need to adapt to your specific circumstances, environment, and situation. With that said, the framework above can be referenced to help however it can best suit you, in each day of your life.

Here are some additional supportive tools when challenges stack up:

- **Anchor practices**: Choose one simple action, like humming, drinking a glass of water, wiggling your toes, placing a hand on your heart, or going outside to ground you.

- **Micro-decisions**: When overwhelmed, don't try to tackle your entire to-do list. Rather than trying to fix all the problems simultaneously, focus on addressing the top item on the list. Take just the *next* step, rather than planning the entire journey.

- **Self-talk reset**: Notice how you are speaking to yourself. If you are critical or harsh, try reframing your speech to the way you would address a child or a close friend.

Your strength is not measured by overcoming storms. It's measured by how you stand by your values within them. Being able to respond the way you intend to, is deeply impacted by how much care you show yourself while you are inside these storms. Let your feathers get ruffled and let your plans change. Let yourself rest when you need to. Know that when life feels challenging, you haven't lost your flight, you're simply learning how to fly through different environments.

In the next chapter, we'll explore what it means to make your world your own. This means living with freedom, truth, and authenticity. You weren't meant to stay in someone else's cage, or even in your own cage built for protection. You were meant to soar as yourself.

Chapter 10: A Sky of Your Own

At some point in your journey, life becomes less about healing what caged you, and more about discovering and aligning to what frees you. That's where this final chapter leads us: *flying into your own sky*.

Birds don't ask for permission to fly. They don't compare wings or migration patterns of other species. They listen to their own instincts, intuition, and follow what feels true to them. You're allowed to live this way too.

For too long you may have been trying to fit in, please others, or live up to expectations that never fully resonated with you. Real lightness comes when you begin to claim your own space and recognize that you don't have to follow a map someone else drew. This doesn't mean others have to support your path, it's up to you to determine this for yourself. This also means finding peace in living by your own free will, rather than needing acknowledgement about your choices from other people.

Living like a bird isn't just about emotional regulation or resilience. It's about *being real*. Making choices rooted in your values, your voice, your vision for life. It's about asking questions like:

- If I am to wake up and start creating my life, what kind of life do I want to build?
- What have I been quieting or denying to make others comfortable?
- What inside me is ready to shine?

Your space in the sky might look different than someone else's. That's not just okay, it's essential. Not all skies are the same, and a flock doesn't thrive by all being identical. Like each snowflake is unique, each bird is unique, as are we. We are just the main species who tend to be critical or feel judged for our differences. While nature may not overthink, it can still be harsh. But as humans, we have the capacity to choose compassion and love towards each other and ourselves.

Now you've done the work to breathe, investigate, redirect, and decide. You can carry this skillset forward and reference it anytime throughout your life. As you begin weathering the storms with more perspective and reclaim more of your joy, what's left is space. This spaciousness is meant to live in, to be, to choose, and to sing. Let that space be yours. Use this space to continue practicing curiosity by asking questions like:

- How do you want to move, speak, and show up?
- How have things changed since you started your practice living the BIRD Way?
- How would you like them to change from here?

The sky is not a destination. It's a wide-open canvas with space for you. You don't have to become someone else to fly, you simply must return to who you really are. Choose to live as yourself and let that truth carry you.

The foundation of the BIRD Way is to let the song of the birds reach your heart and *live with love.*

Conclusion

If you've made it this far, you've done more than just read a book. You've taken steps in a new direction. You don't have to keep thinking about birds to retain the message that you are empowered to create what you desire. I do hope you will continue to Breathe, Investigate, Redirect, and Decide what you want to do with this life.

The BIRD Way is about returning authority to yourself, to create more self-control and responsibility in your life. This can happen even after it might have gotten lost under stories or distractions. It's remembering your breath when the world feels tight, turning inward with compassion and light. It's loosening your grip on resistance and habits while deciding the way to build your practice.

Your life doesn't have to feel so heavy. Your inner world can become a place where clarity and calm are more natural. You don't have to do it all at once; you just need to start where you are now. Every breath, every shift in focus, every commitment, is a weight lifted. As these changes compound, you will become lighter than you were before.

So, carry the BIRD Way with you. Practice it when life feels heavy, and even more when it doesn't. Let it support you in how you respond, how you lead, and how you live.

Flight

I stood with the edge of the sky on my chest,
the wind like a whisper, unsure of the rest.
My feathers were shaking, my legs full of doubt,
Was I made for the sky or this branch holding out?

A hush held my wings in the cradle of air,
and I listened inside, was the courage still there?
I followed the tremble, the flutter, the beat,
and wondered what waited below my own feet.

A moment. A breath. A pause held me still,
I leaned into questions being asked by my will.
Could I land if I fall? And what if I rise?
What if the wind is just truth in disguise?

I turned from the stories that had tied down my beak,
and faced the soft call that invited the leap.
Not all was certain, not all was clear,
but I chose to move closer, going right through my fear.

And so, I let go, not of all that I knew,
but of needing a map in exchange for the view.
My wings were not perfect, my landing alright,
but the sky promised me: you'll grow once you take flight.

Thank You

I hope this book helps lead you towards more lightness, discernment, and joy in your life.

You can share these ideas with others by leaving a review:

With gratitude,

Forest of Truth

Feeling lighter? Want to keep the message close?

If so, check out our
100% organic cotton t-shirts, inspired by *The BIRD Way*:

www.ingramcontent.com/pod-product-compliance
Lightning Source LLC
Chambersburg PA
CBHW070045070426
42449CB00012BA/3167